Content

C000133350

Great Sport Relief Bake Off Introduction

Welcome to your Great Sport Relief Bake Off booklet. By purchasing this little treat, you have already donated £2 to help change lives. **Thank you.**

The following ingredients were used to make your booklet: a smattering of scrumptious recipes, a spoonful of helpful baking advice and a huge dollop of love. Plus, some tasty bake sale tips to help you raise a fortune for Sport Relief.

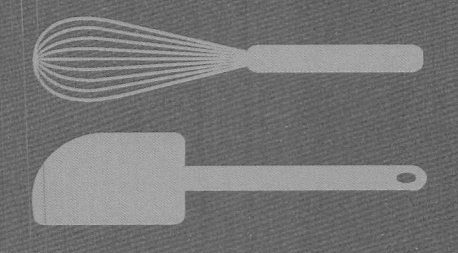

All the delicious recipes have been taken from Bake Off books. But you don't have to be a star baker to make them. In fact, they're as easy as pie but they're not all pies (though pies are very yummy and we wouldn't say no if you made us one).

And the sweetest bit of all is the money you raise goes to helping people living incredibly tough lives in the UK and across the world's poorest communities.

So, rolling pins at the ready!
On your marks, get set, bake yourself proud for Sport Relief.

P.S. If you want an extra serving of fundraising recipes and handy tools; like bunting, cake labels and a poster, download our free Great Sport Relief Bake Off Kit at sportrelief.com/bakeoffkit

How to hold a showstopping bake sale

These handy tips will have you serving up a delicious bake sale for Sport Relief in no time.

1 Ask friends, colleagues and family to join you. They could bake a few treats or help out on the day.

2 Pick a venue that you can use for free – your home, work, local sports centre, place of worship or community hall.

3 Once you've got a venue, make sure you set the date to avoid double bookings.

4 Time your bake sale for when people will want a nibble – during break times, lunch or afternoon tea.

5 Tell everyone about your bake sale in advance! Have a look at the Promote your Fundraising Guide at sportrelief.com/promote. Use the poster in the Bake Off Kit to advertise your bake sale.

6 Make sure you've got sandwich bags or containers so everyone can take their cakes away.

7 Raise a little extra by selling tea and coffee with your cakes and soft drinks for the little ones.

8 Have a list of ingredients for people with allergies and label your nut-free or gluten-free bakes.

9 Bring enough spare change and make your cake prices round numbers to make things easier.

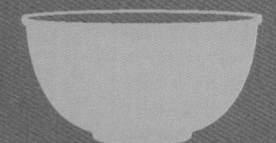

Bake yourself proud

The money you raise will help people living incredibly tough lives. Half the money raised by the public is spent right here in the UK, with the other half used to make a difference in the world's poorest communities. **Thank you.**

£50 could pay for a young person in the UK with a disability to take part in 10 sports sessions.

£80 could provide a loan for a family living in poverty in Nepal to start up their own business, helping them generate more income so they can send their children to school.

£130 could buy all the books, toys and learning materials needed to set up a nursery in rural Ghana, helping to give hundreds of children an education and a brighter future.

Oatmeal Raisin Cookies

These cookies may be loaded with good stuff but are still deliciously sweet and chewy. Use whole rolled oats for a better flavour and texture rather than quick-cook porridge oats.

Makes: 30 biscuits

225g unsalted butter, at room temperature

200g soft light brown sugar

50g soft dark brown sugar

1 teaspoon vanilla extract

2 large eggs, lightly beaten

175g plain flour

1 teaspoon bicarbonate of soda

½ teaspoon ground cinnamon

good pinch of salt

200g rolled porridge oats

150g raisins

100g pecans, roughly chopped

50g desiccated coconut

50g mixed seeds (sunflower, pumpkin, sesame and golden linseed)

1. Cream the butter with the light and dark brown sugars in a free-standing mixer until pale and light – this will take about 3 minutes. Scrape down the insides of the bowl from time to time so that all of the ingredients are thoroughly incorporated. Add the vanilla extract and mix again.

2. Gradually add the beaten eggs, mixing well between each addition. Sift the flour, bicarbonate of soda, ground cinnamon and a good pinch of salt into the bowl and mix until barely combined. Add the oats, raisins, chopped pecans, coconut and seeds and mix again until all of the ingredients are thoroughly incorporated. Cover the bowl with clingfilm and chill for 1 hour.

3. Preheat the oven to 180°C (160°C fan) /350°F/ Gas 4 and line two baking sheets with baking paper.

4. Scoop level tablespoons of dough into balls and place on the prepared baking sheets, leaving plenty of space between each one to allow for spreading during cooking. Flatten each cookie with your hands and bake in batches on the middle shelf of the oven for 12–14 minutes, until crisp and golden brown. The cookies are better when slightly soft and chewy, and as they crisp up as they cool, don't overcook them.

5. Remove from the oven and leave on the baking sheets for 2–3 minutes to firm up, then transfer the cookies to a wire cooling rack using a palette knife or fish slice. These cookies can be rolled into balls and frozen in bags, then baked from frozen or defrosted first.

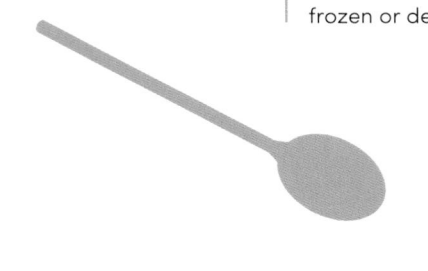

Quick Berry Muffins

These lovely and easy fresh fruit muffins are a great way to practise making a creamed cake mixture. It's a simple way to add lightness to a bake that you'll use again and again.

Makes: 12 muffins

60g unsalted butter, softened

150g caster sugar

1 medium unwaxed lemon

2 medium eggs, at room temperature

275g self-raising flour

½ teaspoon bicarbonate of soda

125ml natural yoghurt (unsweetened, not Greek-style)

200g fresh blueberries or raspberries

2 tablespoons coarse sugar crystals, for sprinkling

1. Preheat the oven to 200°C (180°C fan) /400°F/ Gas 6. Line a 12-hole cupcake tray or muffin tray with paper cases.

2. Put the butter into a mixing bowl or the bowl of a food-mixer and beat well with a wooden spoon or the whisk attachment until the mixture is creamy. Gradually beat in the caster sugar, scraping down the bowl every now and then. Finely grate the zest of the lemon into the bowl and beat it in.

3. Break the eggs into a separate bowl and beat them with a fork until broken up, then beat into the mixing bowl, a tablespoon at a time, until the mixture is quite soft.

4. Sift the flour and bicarbonate of soda into the bowl and stir in with a plastic spatula or wooden spoon.

5. Squeeze 1 tablespoon of juice from the lemon and stir this into the yoghurt, then stir this into the muffin mixture. As soon as it is thoroughly combined, add the fresh blueberries or raspberries to the bowl and gently fold in so the fruit does not break up.

6. Spoon the mixture into the paper cases, dividing it equally so that they are equally filled, then sprinkle over the coarse sugar crystals.

7. Bake for 20–25 minutes until golden brown. Check that the centres of the muffins feel firm when gently pressed. Set the tray on a wire rack and leave the muffins to cool in the tray for 5 minutes, then lift them out of the tray and onto the wire rack to cool. Eat warm or at room temperature on the day you baked them.

Dairy-free Citrus & Spelt Cake

For lemon drizzle fans, a moist loaf cake packed with flavour is perfect for any celebration. This one is made with white spelt flour and a light olive oil instead of butter – the oil should be mild enough to add to the lovely fruity taste of the sponge without overpowering it. As usual the drizzle comes from quickly made lemon water-icing, spread over the cake while still hot.

Makes: 1 large cake

FOR THE SPONGE

4 medium eggs,
at room temperature

225g caster sugar

finely grated zest of
1 large orange, plus 2
tablespoons juice

finely grated zest of
1 large unwaxed lemon,
plus 1 tablespoon juice

225ml mild, fruity extra
virgin olive oil

250g white spelt flour

½ teaspoon baking
powder

½ teaspoon bicarbonate
of soda

FOR THE ICING

100g icing sugar

2–3 tablespoons lemon
juice

1. Heat the oven to 180°C (160°C fan) /350°F/ Gas 4. Break the eggs into a large mixing bowl, or the bowl of a large free-standing electric mixer. Add the sugar and orange and lemon zests. Whisk, using a handheld electric whisk or the whisk attachment of the mixer, on full speed for about 8 minutes.

2. Gradually whisk in the orange and lemon juices, then slowly add the oil in a thin, steady stream, still whisking on full speed – the mixture will become thinner and much less foamy. Sift the flour, baking powder and bicarbonate of soda into the bowl and gently but thoroughly fold in using a large metal spoon or plastic spatula until you can no longer see any specks of flour.

3. Pour the mixture into a greased, lined 900g loaf tin and ease it into the corners so it is evenly filled. Bake in the heated oven for 50–55 minutes until the cake is golden brown and a skewer inserted into the centre comes out clean.

4. While the cake is baking make the lemon water-icing. Sift the icing sugar into a bowl, add the lemon juice and stir to make a smooth, runny icing.

5. When the cake is ready, take the tin out of the oven and set it on a wire rack. Spoon the lemon icing over the top of the hot cake and gently spread out evenly with an offset palette knife or a round-bladed knife. Leave to cool completely.

6. Run a round-bladed knife around the inside of the tin to loosen the cake, then carefully lift it out using the ends of the lining paper to help. Keep in an airtight container and eat within 4 days.

Flapjacks

These flapjacks are delicious and moreish and have a crunchier texture with the addition of mixed seeds. For your perfect flapjack – crunchy or chewy – follow the timings below.

Makes: 16 squares

100g golden syrup

100g demerara sugar

125g unsalted butter, diced

250g rolled porridge oats

75g mixed seeds (sunflower, pumpkin, golden linseed and sesame)

¼ teaspoon ground ginger

pinch of salt

1. Preheat the oven to 180°C (160°C fan) /350°F/ Gas 4 and line the base and sides of a 20cm square baking tin with baking paper.

2. To make it easy to measure golden syrup from a tin, first heat a tablespoon in a mug of boiling water for a minute before using. If you have digital scales, place a small pan on the scales, making sure they are registering zero, and use the hot spoon to scoop the syrup from the tin and into the pan. Re-set the scales to zero and add the demerara sugar and unsalted butter. Set the pan over a low heat to melt the butter and dissolve the sugar. Stir until smooth and remove from the heat.

3. Mix the porridge oats, mixed seeds, ginger and salt in a mixing bowl. Add the melted butter mixture and stir well to thoroughly combine. Spoon into the prepared tin and press level with the back of a spoon.

4. Bake on the middle shelf of the oven for 20–25 minutes, until starting to firm, remembering to use the shorter cooking time for more chewy flapjacks and the longer time if you prefer them crisper. The flapjacks will firm up and crisp as they cool.

5. Remove from the oven and mark the flapjack into squares. Cool in the tin on a wire rack.

Double Chocolate Peanut Butter Cookies

These delicious cookies are packed with dark and white chocolate chunks and a double dose of peanuts. The trick is not to overbake them so they are slightly soft in the middle.

Makes: 24 biscuits

125g dark chocolate, preferably a minimum of 65 per cent cocoa solids, chopped

125g white chocolate

100g salted roasted peanuts

100g unsalted butter, at room temperature

125g crunchy peanut butter

225g soft light brown sugar

2 large eggs, lightly beaten

1 teaspoon vanilla extract

200g plain flour

40g cocoa powder

1 teaspoon bicarbonate of soda

½ teaspoon baking powder

pinch of salt

2 tablespoons milk

1. Preheat the oven to 170°C (150°C fan) /340°F/ Gas 3 and line two baking sheets with baking paper.

2. Melt the dark chocolate in a heatproof glass or ceramic bowl over a pan of barely simmering water, making sure the bottom of the bowl doesn't touch the water. Stir until smooth, remove from the heat and leave to cool slightly. Chop the white chocolate into chunks and very roughly chop the peanuts and put to one side.

3. Cream the butter with the peanut butter and soft light brown sugar until pale and light – this will be easiest using a free-standing mixer fitted with the creamer/paddle attachment. Gradually add the eggs, mixing well between each addition and scraping down the sides of the bowl with a rubber spatula from time to time. Add the vanilla extract and mix again.

4. Add the cooled melted chocolate and mix until smooth. Sift the flour, cocoa powder, bicarbonate of soda, baking powder and a pinch of salt into the bowl and mix until barely combined before adding the milk, white chocolate chunks and chopped peanuts. Mix again to thoroughly combine.

5. Using a tablespoon, scoop even-sized mounds onto the lined baking sheets, leaving plenty of space between each cookie to allow them to spread during baking. Bake in batches, for 10 minutes on the middle shelf of the oven. Remove from the oven and flatten each cookie slightly with a fish slice or palette knife and return to the oven for a further minute. The cookies will still be slightly soft at this point but will harden as they cool – if you can wait that long. Cool the cookies on the baking sheets for a few minutes and then transfer to a wire rack to cool completely.

Salt 'n' Peppered Sausage Rolls

The perfect picnic or party food, sausage rolls are incredibly easy to make, especially when using bought puff pastry.

Makes: 16 sausage rolls

1 teaspoon olive or rapeseed oil

1 shallot, finely chopped

1 garlic clove, finely chopped

400g good-quality pork sausages (about 6 sausages)

3 tablespoons fresh white breadcrumbs

¼ teaspoon English mustard powder

1 rounded teaspoon finely chopped sage leaves

300g bought puff pastry block

beaten egg, to glaze

sea salt flakes and freshly ground black pepper

1. Heat the oil in a small non-stick frying pan. Tip in the shallot and garlic clove and fry for about 3 minutes, until softened and only lightly coloured. Leave to cool.

2. Squeeze the sausage meat out of the skins of the sausages into a bowl. Mix in the cooled shallot, the breadcrumbs, mustard powder and chopped sage leaves and season with pepper. You shouldn't need to add salt as the sausage meat is salty and you will be sprinkling some on the pastry later.

3. Preheat the oven to 190°C (170°C fan) /375°F/ Gas 5. Line a large baking sheet with baking paper. Roll out the bought puff pastry on a lightly floured surface and trim to a 37 × 23cm rectangle, then cut in half lengthways. Halve the sausage mixture and shape both halves into a 37cm long roll by rolling and pressing it into shape. Flour your hands and work surface well for this stage.

4. Lay one of the pastry strips on a lightly floured board. Place a roll of sausage meat mixture down one long side. Brush the far long side of pastry with beaten egg. Roll the pastry over the sausage meat to enclose it completely. Where the pastry joins, press well to seal and then knock back the edges by tapping into the pastry with the back of a small sharp knife to make small slash marks. Make sure the seal is tight otherwise the sausage meat will pop out as the rolls bake. Roll it over so the join is underneath. With a sharp knife, cut the roll into eight equal pieces, reshaping if necessary. Repeat with the rest of your sausage mixture.

5. Place the rolls on the baking sheet, with the joins underneath. Make three or four slash marks on top of each roll with a sharp knife, brush them with beaten egg to glaze and sprinkle them with pepper and a few small sea salt flakes. Bake for 25–30 minutes, or until golden, puffy and the meat is cooked through. Remove and cool slightly before serving fresh and warm, but they are also good cold.

Carrot Spice Cake

Always popular, this classic carrot cake is quick to put together and has a delightful combination of creamy Carrot Spice Cake and crunchy textures.

Makes: 1 large cake

FOR THE SPONGE

230g self-raising flour

1 teaspoon baking powder

1½ teaspoons ground cinnamon

¼ teaspoon grated nutmeg

½ teaspoon ground ginger

½ teaspoon ground mixed spice

200g caster sugar

100g walnut pieces, plus 1 tablespoon finely chopped for topping

3 medium eggs

150ml sunflower oil

500g carrots, coarsely grated

FOR THE CREAM CHEESE FROSTING

1 large unwaxed lime

200g full-fat cream cheese

50g unsalted butter, softened

150g icing sugar

1. Preheat the oven to 180°C (160°C fan) /350°F/ Gas 4. Grease and line 2 x 20.5cm round sandwich cake tins with butter and baking paper.

2. To make the sponge, sift the self-raising flour, baking powder, ground cinnamon, grated nutmeg, ground ginger and ground mixed spice into a large bowl. Add the caster sugar and walnuts and mix with a wooden spoon.

3. In a separate bowl, add the eggs to the sunflower oil and beat lightly with a fork. Pour into the dry ingredients, tip in the grated carrots and mix again. Divide the carrot mixture equally between the two prepared cake tins – if you want to be really accurate, use your scales, or you can just do it by eye.

4. Bake for 25–30 minutes until the cakes are golden and a cocktail stick or skewer inserted into the centre comes out clean. Turn out the cakes onto a wire rack, carefully peeling off the lining paper, then leave them until cold.

5. While the cakes are cooling, make the cream cheese frosting. Finely grate the lime zest into a mixing bowl, squeeze in 1½ teaspoons of the lime juice and add the cream cheese and butter. Sift the icing sugar over the top then beat everything together with an electric whisk until the mixture is smooth, creamy and spreadable. If it is a warm day or your kitchen is hot, cover the bowl at this point and pop it in the fridge to chill for a couple of minutes to thicken up the frosting.

6. Now put your cake together. Flip one sponge so it's top-side down on a serving plate and spread it with half the cream cheese frosting. Pop the second sponge on top and spread it with the rest of the frosting using a roundbladed or palette knife. You don't need to make a perfectly neat finish, but it looks nice with a little swirl made with a flick of the knife at the end. Finally, scatter the finely chopped walnuts around the edge.

White Chocolate Butterscotch Blondies

Scrumptious little squares to make for parties or just for a treat, these are called blondies because they are made with white chocolate rather than the dark chocolate used in brownies. They're topped with fresh raspberries, which add a flash of flavour and colour. The mixture is very easy to make – everything combined in a saucepan.
Be sure to use a good-quality white chocolate.

Makes: 16 blondies

115g unsalted butter

115g dark brown muscovado sugar

1 medium egg, at room temperature

½ teaspoon vanilla extract

150g plain flour

2 good pinches of salt

½ teaspoon bicarbonate of soda

100g good-quality white chocolate (at least 30% cocoa solids), broken up

100g fresh raspberries

1. Preheat the oven to 180°C (160°C fan) /350°F/ Gas 4. Grease and line a 20.5cm square tin.

2. Put the butter in a medium pan and set over low heat. When the butter has melted, turn up the heat to medium and leave the butter to bubble until it is golden with darker speckles (don't stand too close as the butter may spit). Remove from the heat and add the sugar. Stir with a wooden spoon until thoroughly mixed and lump-free. The mixture will look a bit of a mess at this stage, but don't worry! Leave to cool for 5 minutes.

3. Meanwhile, break the egg into a small bowl or cup, add the vanilla extract and beat with a fork until combined.

4. Add the egg to the butter mixture and stir well with the wooden spoon. Sift the flour, salt and bicarbonate of soda into the pan and mix in. Finally, add the broken-up chocolate to the pan and mix until evenly distributed.

5. Transfer the mixture to the prepared tin and spread evenly, making sure the corners are evenly filled. Top with the raspberries, setting them pointed end up on top of the mixture.

6. Bake in the heated oven for about 25 minutes until a skewer inserted into the blondie cake halfway between one side and the centre comes out clean (the centre will still be soft but the mixture will continue cooking for a few minutes after it comes out of the oven).

7. Set the tin on a wire rack. Run a round-bladed knife around the inside of the tin to loosen the blondie cake, then leave until cold before cutting into squares and removing from the tin. Best eaten the same or the next day – store the blondies in an airtight container in a cool spot.

Vanilla Traybake

A traybake is a simple no-fuss all-in-one mixture. It uses just a few ingredients you probably already have, but can be glammed up with anything from glittery sprinkles to silver balls.

Makes: 20 squares

FOR THE SPONGE

125g unsalted butter, softened

125g caster sugar

1 teaspoon vanilla extract

2 medium eggs, at room temperature, beaten

1 tablespoon milk, at room temperature

150g self-raising flour

FOR THE FROSTING

250g icing sugar

100g unsalted butter, softened

1 tablespoon milk

½ teaspoon vanilla extract, or to taste

decorations of your choice

1. Preheat the oven to 180°C (160°C fan) /350°F/ Gas 4. Grease and line a 25.5 x 20.5 x 5cm tin with butter and baking paper.

2. To make the sponge, put the butter, sugar, vanilla, eggs, milk and flour into a large bowl or the bowl of a food-mixer. Beat everything together with a spoon or the whisk attachment. Start slowly – otherwise the mixture could fly out of the bowl – and scrape down the sides of the bowl every now and then with a spatula. After about 2 minutes the mixture should look very smooth and light. If you are adding any flavourings or other ingredients, stir them in now.

3. Scrape the mixture into the prepared tin and spread it out right into the corners, making sure it is nice and even. Bake for 20–25 minutes until the top is a good golden brown. You can check your cake is cooked by gently pressing the centre lightly with your fingertips; it should spring back.

4. Stand the tin on a wire rack and run a round-bladed knife around the inside to loosen the sponge. Leave it to cool and firm up in the tin and it will be easier to remove. When cooled, turn out the cake and peel off the paper.

5. While the sponge is cooling, make the frosting. Sift the icing sugar into a mixing bowl then add the butter, milk and vanilla extract and beat well with a spoon or electric whisk on a low speed until the frosting is smooth and light.

6. Swirl the icing over the top of the cold sponge with a palette knife. If you want to decorate the top, do it now before the icing firms up. Cut into squares to serve.

Mini Bakewells with Fresh Raspberries

These classic Bakewell tarts are a great way to move on to making rich shortcrust pastry. The trick is not to overfill the tart cases, so the filling stays neat and rounded as it bakes.

Makes: 12 tarts

FOR THE RICH SHORTCRUST PASTRY

175g plain flour
95g chilled butter, diced
1 teaspoon icing sugar
1 medium egg yolk

FOR THE ALMOND FILLING

50g butter, at room temperature
50g golden caster sugar
2 medium eggs, beaten
50g ground almonds
few drops of almond extract
2 tablespoons raspberry jam
12 raspberries
a handful of flaked almonds

1. Put the flour, butter and icing sugar into a large bowl. Rub in until the mixture looks like fine breadcrumbs. Drop in the egg yolk and about 1 tablespoon of cold water (add a bit more if needed to bring the dough together) and stir it in with a round-bladed knife to form a dough. Gently work the dough together into a smooth ball with your hands, being careful not to over handle the dough. Shape the dough into a thick disc, wrap in clingfilm and chill in the fridge for 15–20 minutes, until firm but not hard.

2. Roll out the dough on a lightly floured surface to about the thickness of a £1 coin. Use the round pastry cutter to cut out circles. Gather up the leftover pieces of pastry, re-roll and cut out more until you have 12. Line each hole of a 12-hole bun tin with the pastry circles and then chill them for 15 minutes while you prepare the almond filling. Preheat the oven to 190°C (170°C fan) /375°F/ Gas 5.

3. Beat the butter and sugar with a wooden spoon until fluffy and paler in colour. Start to beat in the eggs a little at a time, beating well between each addition. Don't worry if the mixture looks curdled right now – it will all come together when you add the ground almonds. Stir in the ground almonds and almond extract (the mixture will be quite runny).

4. Spoon ½ teaspoon of the jam into the bottom of each pastry circle. Now spoon enough of the almond filling into each tart case to almost fill. Don't be tempted to overfill or the mixture will bubble over as it bakes. Sit a raspberry in the middle and press it lightly into the filling, but not all the way down. Scatter a few flaked almonds around each raspberry.

5. Bake for 20 minutes, until pale golden on top and the pastry is cooked. Cool slightly and transfer to a wire rack to cool completely.

Simple & Pretty Fruitcake

A moist and light 'cut and come again' fruitcake that uses the very forgiving rubbed-in method, which makes it a perfect fruitcake for first-time bakers to make.

Makes: 1 large cake

FOR THE SPONGE

350g self-raising flour

good pinch of salt

175g unsalted butter, cold and firm (but not hard), diced

175g golden caster sugar

finely grated zest of 1 unwaxed lemon

275g luxury mixed fruit

150g marzipan, cut into 1.5cm cubes

3 medium eggs, at room temperature

4 tablespoons milk, at room temperature

FOR THE TOPPING

2 tablespoons apricot jam, sifted, or apricot glaze

2 teaspoons boiling water

2 tablespoons toasted flaked almonds

1. Preheat the oven to 180°C (160°C fan) /350°F/ Gas 4. Grease and line a 20.5cm deep round cake tin with baking paper.

2. To make the sponge, sift the flour and salt into a mixing bowl, then add the butter, tossing it in the flour to coat. Using the very tips of your fingers, rub in the butter with the flour until the mixture looks like fine crumbs. Stir in the golden caster sugar and lemon zest with a wooden spoon. When everything is combined, add the mixed fruit and marzipan and mix well.

3. Beat the eggs and milk in a small bowl with a fork until just combined, then tip them into the mixing bowl and stir well with the spoon until you have a stiff mixture. Scrape the mixture into the prepared tin and spread evenly.

4. Bake for 70 minutes until golden brown. Check your cake is cooked by inserting a cocktail stick or skewer into the centre; if it comes out clean, it is ready. You might need to test in several places to avoid hitting a lump of marzipan, though!

5. Set the tin on a wire rack, run a round-bladed knife around the inside of the tin to loosen the cake, then unclip the sides. Leave on the rack until cold.

6. To make the topping, mix the jam with the boiling water until smooth, then brush it over the cake. Scatter over the almonds and leave to set for 20 minutes.

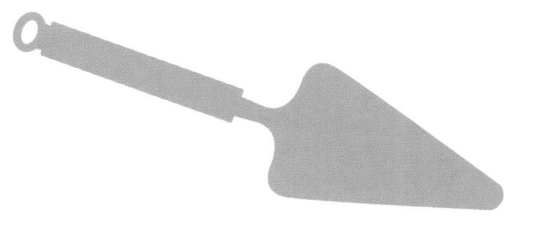

Thumbprint Cookies

These crumbly cookies couldn't be easier, with no fancy cutters or rolling out. Try swapping 15g of the plain flour for the same amount of cocoa powder and fill the indent with chocolate spread.

200g unsalted butter, at room temperature

100g caster sugar

1 large egg yolk

1 teaspoon vanilla extract

275g plain flour

pinch of salt

150g raspberry jam

1. Cream together the butter and caster sugar until really pale and light – you'll find this easiest using a freestanding mixer fitted with the creamer/paddle attachment but a hand-held mixer or bowl and wooden spoon will do just as well. Scrape down the sides of the bowl with a rubber spatula from time to time as you are working.

2. Add the egg yolk and vanilla extract and mix again until thoroughly combined. Sift the flour into the bowl with the salt and mix until the dough comes together into a smooth ball. Don't overwork the dough or the cookies could end up tough rather than crisp and crumbly. Cover the bowl with clingfilm and chill for 1 hour, until firm.

3. Preheat the oven to 180°C (160°C fan) /350°F/ Gas 4 and line two baking sheets with baking paper. Using your hands, roll the dough into walnut-sized balls and arrange on the lined baking sheets, leaving a little space between each biscuit, as they will spread slightly during cooking.

4. Using your thumb or finger, press into the middle of each cookie. Bake on the middle shelf of the oven for about 15 minutes, or until pale golden. Remove from the oven and gently press your thumb into the indent again. Fill each indent with ½–1 teaspoon of jam, depending on its depth, and return the cookies to the oven for another minute.

5. Leave to cool on the baking sheet for a few minutes, then transfer to a wire rack to cool completely.

Double Chocolate Cupcakes

Using oil instead of butter in this super-speedy cupcake recipe means you don't have to cream the mixture.

FOR THE SPONGE

140g self-raising flour

40g cocoa powder

good pinch of salt

200g caster sugar

125ml sunflower oil

1 medium egg, at room temperature

175ml milk, at room temperature

1 teaspoon vanilla extract

100g white chocolate chips (or milk or dark)

FOR THE FROSTING

75g icing sugar

25g cocoa powder

50g unsalted butter

50g caster sugar

2 tablespoons milk

extra chocolate chips, to decorate

1. Preheat the oven to 190°C (170°C fan) /375°F/ Gas 5. Line a 12-hole cupcake tray with paper cases.

2. Put the flour, cocoa powder, salt and sugar into the food-processor bowl fitted with the blade. Pulse 3–4 times until everything is thoroughly mixed. (If you don't have a food-processor make the cakes using the traditional all-in-one whisking method, it just takes a bit longer.)

3. Pour the sunflower oil into a jug with the egg, milk and vanilla extract and beat everything together with a fork until the egg is broken up.

4. Switch on the food-processor and pour the liquid through the feed tube with the machine running. Once it is all added, stop the machine, scrape down the bowl, then pulse again for 10 seconds, until the mixture is smooth, creamy and streak-free.

5. Remove the blade and stir the chocolate chips into the cake mix using a plastic spatula. Divide the mixture between the paper cases so they are half filled.

6. Bake for 18–20 minutes. Check the cakes after 15 minutes and if they aren't cooking evenly, rotate the tray. They are ready when they spring back when you gently press them in the centre. Carefully remove from the tray and cool on a wire rack.

7. To make the frosting, sift the icing sugar and cocoa into a heatproof bowl. Melt the butter with the sugar and milk in a small pan over a low heat, stir well, then bring to the boil. Once boiling, immediately pour the mixture over the icing sugar and cocoa. Mix until smooth. Leave for 10 minutes until thickened and spreadable.

8. Swirl the frosting over the cooled cupcakes using a round-bladed knife or an offset palette knife. Scatter over the extra chocolate chips before the frosting sets.

Huge thanks to everyone who helped put this book together

Rita Platts, David Munns, Amanda Heywood, Mark Bourdillion, Victoria Dawe, Lucille Flood, Brian Sokol, Simon Vine, Anna Beattie, Rupert Frisby, Jane Treasure, Claire Emerson, James Hedge, Nicky Ross, Sarah Hammond, Lauren Whelan, Mark Read, Claudette Morris, Bobby Birchall, and special thanks to the Comic Relief Team.

First published in Great Britain in 2016 by Hodder & Stoughton
An Hachette UK company

1

Recipes by Linda Collister, Annie Rigg, and Angela Nilsen
© Love Productions

Photography by Rita Platts, David Munns, and Amanda Heywood
© Hodder & Stoughton, except page 2 © Victoria Dawe, and page 5 © Simon Vine, Brian Sokol and Victoria Dawe.

Design by Bobby Birchall, Bobby&Co

All the recipes from this booklet were taken from *The Great British Bake Off: Celebrations, Great British Bake Off – Bake it Better (No.1): Classic Cakes, Great British Bake Off – Bake it Better (No.2): Biscuits, Great British Bake Off – Bake it Better (No.3): Pies & Tarts*

A CIP catalogue record for this title is available from the British Library

ISBN 978 1 473 63174 8

Printed and bound in Germany by GGP Media GmbH, Pößneck

Hodder & Stoughton policy is to use papers that are natural, renewable and recyclable products and made from wood grown in sustainable forests. The logging and manufacturing processes are expected to conform to the environmental regulations of the country of origin.

Hodder & Stoughton Ltd
Carmelite House
50 Victoria Embankment
London EC4Y 0DZ

www.hodder.co.uk

COMIC RELIEF   **LOVE** productions   **HODDER & STOUGHTON**

Sport Relief is an initiative of Comic Relief, registered charity 326568 (England Wales); SCO39730 (Scotland)